MW01122873

Girls Are Like Pizza

"Every slice counts"
A Guide to Sexual Purity

Fawn Nole

ISBN-13: 978-1523203567 (softcover)
ISBN-10: 1523203560 (e-book)

I dedicate this book to my two beautiful children, Daniel and Kate. May God guide you as you grow into young adults, and wait on the Lord to bless you with the one He has set aside, just for you.

Contents

Introduction

You may be asking, "What's up with the title?" Let me explain: Think of your sexual life as a pizza that has about eight slices. We're talking hypothetically. I'm sure you will agree that most guys love pizza. Well, before we're married we go through a lot of changes. Our moods, our minds, and our bodies begin to change. It seems as though girls go through more dramatic changes than boys, but trust me, there are probably equal amounts taking place. Among these are hormonal changes; the subject most people don't want to talk about. Aside from the pimples, frizzy hair, weight gain and growth spurts, we begin to feel differently towards the opposite sex. Now, if we were to act on those feelings and jump into a relationship where there are no boundaries, we would be opening doors that should not be opened until marriage. More times than not teens partake in sexual activity before marriage because of the following: out of control hormones (yes, they can be controlled), no boundaries (adult supervision) and carelessness (they don't care enough about themselves to abstain from sexual activity).

As a girl, if you were to give away one of your "slices" to a guy before marriage, what would you have left? Seven slices? Maybe, but you'd also have an empty space. If you continue to give away slices, whether they are to the same guy or others, you will continue to have empty spaces until you have nothing left to give to your future spouse. We'll take this analogy a little deeper later on when I talk about what happens after your box is empty.

My story

I grew up in a somewhat "normal" family. My parents are still together to this day which is very rare and I'm very thankful for their strong views on marriage. We always had what we needed and my dad worked hard to provide for us. As I got older, I began to hang out with my friends, stay the night at their houses and eventually go out to events and parties where there was no adult supervision. I had complete freedom by the time I was 13 years old. I began "dating" at the age of 14, which soon led to a serious relationship at the age of 15. I, like many other teens, gave in to my raging hormones and gave away one of those precious "slices" of pizza and soon became pregnant.

Something most people don't know is that this pregnancy wasn't an "unplanned" or "unwanted" pregnancy. I made the choice to get pregnant at such a young age. Why? Because my boyfriend said he loved me and wanted me to have his baby so that we could get married some day. He wanted me to have his baby so he would always be connected to me, no matter where we were in life. I fell for these words that seemed to serenade me into a dream that I wanted so badly to come true.

I gave birth to my son nine days after my 16th birthday; and just like most teen "parents", my relationship with his biological father dwindled away to nothing and I found myself trying to raise my son alone. Thankfully my parents didn't kick me out of the house and they provided for my son and I until I could get out on my own. Before I moved out, I continued to party and give more slices away to guys that didn't care about me until I was completely empty. I began filling those empty spaces with alcohol and drugs. I wanted to stay as numb as possible because I felt empty, dirty, broken and unwanted. I felt like I could never be loved by someone because I had nothing left to give. That's when the mercy and grace of God stepped into my life. He lifted me up out of that dark hole that I had fallen into and turned my life around. Soon I met the man that is now my husband. After we were married, I still dealt with the guilt of my past. For years, I struggled with feeling like I had somehow cheated him out of his blessing because he waited until marriage and I didn't; but God is our Healer. He has miraculously transformed those feelings of guilt and anger into gratitude and peace. I no longer feel negatively about my past because I can teach others how to avoid making the same mistakes I did, and lead sexually, morally and spiritually pure lives.

Slice 1- Why Wait?

As you read earlier, I didn't wait until marriage to have sex. I was 15 years old, and very naive. I believed just about everything, ah who am I kidding, I believed every word that came out of my boyfriends mouth! He told me he loved me and felt like I was "the one" for him. I knew he had been sexually active when I started dating him but I thought I could date someone like him and be strong enough to just say no. Boy, was I wrong. I remember that night very clearly as if it happened just last week. I'll spare you all of the details but it was far from perfect. It happened in an old, run down apartment complex that was previously used as base housing for the military. It was one of those "spur of the moment" things. I had no idea what I was allowing into my life. Would I have waited until marriage if we didn't "hook up" that night? Probably not. But if someone would have talked to me about all of the negative effects of engaging in sexual activity before marriage, I would have at least reconsidered and thought a little harder before giving in.

Society today says, "Waiting for marriage is so old fashioned." Well, they're right; saving yourself for marriage goes way back to the beginning of time. But that doesn't mean we shouldn't wait. Let's look at what the Bible teaches on waiting for marriage. In Genesis chapter 2 God created Adam and He saw that it was not good for man to be alone so He created a woman (Eve) for Adam. And Adam said, "This is now bone of my bones, and flesh of my flesh." If we continue reading in verse 24, it says, "Therefore shall a man leave his father and his mother, and shall cleave unto his wife: and they shall become one flesh."

The Miriam-Webster definition of *cleave* is: to adhere firmly and closely or loyally and unwaveringly.

Sex is the physical act of *cleaving* to one another. When we *cleave* to one another, we are making a lifelong commitment to be "glued" (adhered firmly) to our spouse. Sex is a binding act of love that shows our commitment to each other. It tells the other person you now belong to them and they to you.

As Christians, we want to please God. How do we please God? By following His commandments. In 1 Thessalonians Paul wrote to the Christians who had asked how they should walk and please God. 1 Thessalonians 4:2-5 "*For ye know what commandments we gave you by the Lord Jesus. For this is the will of God, even your sanctification, that ye should abstain from fornication: that every one of you should know how to possess his vessel in sanctification and honour; Not in the lust of concupiscence, even as the Gentiles which know not God:*"

The definition of *Sanctification:* The state of growing in divine grace as a result of Christian commitment after baptism or conversion.

The definition of *Concupiscence:* Strong desire; especially: sexual desire.

In 1 Corinthians chapter 6 verse 9 Paul speaks about those who will not inherit the Kingdom of God: Fornicators, idolaters, adulterers, effeminate, abusers of themselves with mankind, thieves, covetous, drunkards, revilers, or extortioners.

*1 Corinthians 6:18-20 says "Flee fornication.
Every sin that a man doeth is without the
body; but he that committeth fornication
sinneth against his own body. What? Know
ye not that your body is the temple of the
Holy Ghost which is in you, which ye have of
God, and ye are not your own? For ye are
bought with a price: therefore glorify God in
your body, and in your spirit, which are
God's."*

Our bodies are the temple of the Holy
Ghost, so when we decide to abstain from
fornication and lustful desires of the flesh, we
are honoring our bodies, and most
importantly we are honoring God.

*1 Corinthians 7:9 says "But if they cannot
contain, let them marry; for it is better to
marry than to burn."* Contain what? The lust
of the flesh. Obviously, Paul is speaking
about sex before marriage. I can only speak
for myself here, but that scripture alone
would scare me out of having premarital sex!
If, of course, someone had shown it to me
around the age of thirteen.

*Some may laugh and think, "That's extreme"
or "that's taking it too seriously," but God
isn't laughing...He delights in us taking him*

seriously and even more, obeying Him." -
gracepowerstrength.blogspot.com

Sex is so special that it needs a special home; that home is marriage. The ultimate intimacy belongs in the ultimate commitment. -Pat Driscoll

There are so many negative effects premarital sex can cause; it is just simply worth your while to wait until marriage. From unwanted feelings of guilt and pain to STD's and unplanned pregnancies, the negative effects greatly outweigh the positive effects of engaging in sexual activity before marriage. Waiting until marriage will be one of the greatest blessings you could ever give to yourself. It is something that is never remembered with shame or regret, and it always has positive effects that last a lifetime.

Slice 2: Abstaining From Sexual Temptations

Have you ever heard the phrase, "the eyes are the window to the soul?" As a parent, I try to use this phrase to teach my children how to be careful of what they place before their eyes. Once the eyes have seen something they should not have seen, that image does not go away. As a mom, it is one of my greatest fears to think of my children learning of all the horrible, ungodly things that are in the world. I experienced enough to know what is out there, so I feel it is my duty to protect them from it. Unfortunately, I can't be with them at all times, but I can teach them how to keep their eyes on holy things and give them the foundation they need in order to make the right decisions when needed.

Anytime we go out in public there are numerous people dressed immodestly. It is quite difficult to keep our eyes from seeing something that we shouldn't, but there is a difference between seeing something while out and about, or purposefully viewing something that is ungodly and immoral. Also, when we look upon someone with lust in our hearts, we have committed a great sin.

Matthew 5:8 "Blessed are the pure in heart, for they shall see God."

Matthew 5:27-29 "Ye have heard that it was said of them of old time, Thou shalt not commit adultery: But I say unto you, that whosoever looketh on a woman to lust after her hath committed adultery with her already in his heart. And if thy right eye, offend thee, pluck it out and cast it from thee: for it is profitable for thee that one of thy members should perish, and not that thy whole body should be cast into hell."

Ladies, Paul wasn't only speaking to men here. It is easy for women to lust after a man just as it is easy for a man to lust after a woman. There are a lot of attractive men (and women) out there, but that doesn't make it okay to look upon them with a lustful heart.

What exactly is lust? According to good ole Google, lust is a very strong sexual desire. As humans, we were born into sin, but we were given a choice. We can choose to obey God's word and live holy and pure lives, or we can choose to go against God's word and fulfill the desires of our flesh.

Most people have access to social media in some way or another. If you do, it is in your control what you place before your eyes. I enjoy physical exercise so I follow quite a few people on Instagram that are fitness lovers as well. As soon as I see someone posting inappropriate photos, or pictures that show too much skin, whether they be male or female, I decide to no longer follow them. God created us to be attracted to the physical body of the opposite sex, so I want to make sure I don't purposefully view images that could cause me to stumble.

I wasn't always so protective of what I placed before my eyes. I remember using the internet to go into chat rooms and meet boys when I was 13 years old. Most of the time I ended up talking privately to older guys who were only interested in one thing: sex. I saw things I shouldn't have before ever experiencing any kind of sexual activity. When viewing inappropriate images, it awakens something inside of us that shouldn't be awakened until we are ready for marriage. It causes a natural reaction to want to see more and eventually engage in sexual activity, because let's face it, we were born sinners and we are drawn to fleshly desires. The key to abstaining from sexual temptations is staying close to God.

You may be wondering, how do I control those fleshly desires and keep my eyes on the things of God? We must keep our flesh under subjection at all times by reading our Bibles, praying, fasting and being surrounded by pure and holy people. Each of these are extremely important in order to control our thoughts and our actions, but I'd like to put an emphasis on surrounding ourselves with pure and holy people. It is very important to make friends with people who have the same goals, morals and vision in life as you do. We must guard our hearts from worldly things and sometimes this means staying away from certain groups of people. I've had to separate myself from all of my high school friends. I am no longer in touch with any of them. Why? Because they would expose me to my past and could likely cause me to stumble. I have made many friends who are in church as an adult, but I still have to be careful with whom I associate myself with. No one is perfect, but we know what our own struggles and failures are; and surrounding ourselves with like-minded people can only lead to mental, personal and spiritual growth.

Purity is the fruit of prayer. -Mother Teresa

Proverbs 4:23 "Keep thy heart with all diligence; for out of it are the issues of life." The NIV says it this way: "Above all else, guard your heart, for everything you do flows from it."

2 Corinthians 10:5 "...and bringing into captivity every thought to the obedience of Christ."

      Another way to abstain from sexual temptations is to stay busy. Get involved with things like school, sports, extracurricular activities, hobbies and/or outdoor activities. The moment we become idle, we begin to let just about anything entertain us. Arthur Rimbaud said, "*Idle youth, enslaved to everything; by being too sensitive I have wasted my life.*" Such a powerful quote! *Enslaved to everything* when we become too idle with our lives. As a teen, I remember being so bored that whoever called me at that moment and asked me to go do whatever it was they wanted to do, I'd say yes just because I didn't want to be bored anymore.

Talk about a recipe for disaster! Every time my friends and I were bored, we'd figure out a way to get our hands on some alcohol. It seemed like alcohol made life fun, but in reality, it brought on more problems than I needed. How is getting drunk, throwing up, feeling like garbage the following day and remembering very little from the night before fun? I don't remember anything "fun" about those nights. I always regretted the way I behaved and things I said. Get involved with something that brings positivity to your life and try to stay away from becoming too stagnant.

The definition of *stagnant* is: showing no activity; dull or sluggish.
The definition of *idle* is: without purpose or effect; pointless.

1 Timothy 5:13 *"And withal they learn to be idle, wandering about from house to house; and not only idle, but tattlers also and busybodies, speaking things which they ought not."*

Ephesians 5:15-16 *"See then that ye walk circumspectly, not as fools, but as wise, Redeeming the time, because the days are evil."*

When you are truly striving to please God, you will take the time to read His word, to pray and to fast. Seek out friends who have same values in life as you have, remain busy and as always, stay close to the Lord. When you do these things, the Spirit of God that dwells in you will become stronger and your flesh will become weaker, and in time you will have control over your fleshly desires.

Slice 3: Reasons Girls Give in (or even seek out) Sexual Relationships Before Marriage

When I was a little girl, I wanted my daddy's attention more than he realized. He worked hard to provide for our family of six and I knew that was how he showed he loved us; by providing for our everyday needs. What he didn't realize was that as a little girl, I needed more than just clothes on my back and food on the table. I needed to know I was loved by my dad. I needed to know he thought I was special. I longed to hear words like, "you're beautiful" or "I'm so proud of who you are." Instead, he showed his love in how he provided, and although I am forever grateful for his hard work ethic, I still lacked the emotional support I needed solely from my father. I am in no way blaming my dad for not loving me enough as to why I entered into sexual relationships at such a young age; but I have been able to make the connection with longing to be loved by a male figure and not having an adequate amount of emotional support from a father figure while growing up.

As I entered into my teen years, I was given quite a bit of freedom. I was allowed to date, and to be honest, getting the attention from boys made me feel good inside. You all know how my story ended up, but I'd like to share the emotions in between all the dating around, the drinking and the drug abuse. All of these things were "quick fixes". Whenever I was hurting, I'd turn to one of these three things in hopes of filling a void. Did they fill the void? No, they only made me numb for a time. The drinking made life seem not-so-hard. The drugs made life not-so-real. The guys made life seem enjoyable; but only for a time. What happens when those things wear off? You still have pain and you still have a void in your heart. I feel this is how many people get so caught up in drugs because eventually they need more to take the pain away, and then they find themselves out on the street with nothing but their addictions and all the hurt they started with.

The night God changed everything was when I had found out that my son's biological father was going to have a baby with another girl. So what did I do? I went out and became so intoxicated that I still, to this day, do not remember where I went, where I was, or how I got home. By the grace of God, I ended up back at home. I slept for hours straight, so oblivious to life around me. My poor son watched me just lie around and sleep while he played or while my family cared for him. The next night I was lying in bed and I began to cry. I began to feel disgusted with myself. Then I started to pray and repent of all the horrible things I had done. I literally felt like I was in a dark hole that I couldn't get out of. Thankfully, God heard my pleas for help and wrapped His loving arms around me and has never let me go. All those years of trying to fill a void with such wicked things, all I had to do was reach out to my heavenly Father and He was right there to lift me out of that dark hole. He loved me and I never even realized it. All I ever needed was my Father's love and I am forever thankful that He heard my prayer that night.

Isaiah 41:13 "For I the Lord thy God will hold thy right hand, saying unto thee, Fear not; I will help thee."

1 John 4:10 "Herein is love, not that we loved God, but that he loved us, and sent his Son to be the propitiation for our sins."

Some reasons girls engage in sexual relationships before marriage could be they are simply trying to fill a void that only God can fill. They are searching for something that they aren't going to find in any man. They could be searching for self-worth. Especially the girls that look for the "bad boys"; they might feel that they are the missing piece to that person's life and that they are going to fix them and turn them into a good person. Trust me, ladies, there isn't one thing a girl can do to make a "bad boy" good. If a guy can't wait until marriage to be intimate with you, he doesn't have your best interest in heart.

Another reason some girls give into sexual relationships before marriage is because they long to feel wanted and desired. It's natural for a woman to feel this way, but giving away such a precious gift before marriage can only cause harm; emotionally, mentally and physically. Another reason girls tend to have premarital sex is simply because their friends are doing it. I'm guilty of that excuse! I felt like I had to live up to my friends' standards when really I should've been setting the standard for them to follow!

If you place your life in God's hands, He will direct your steps and bless you with the man you deserve, in His time. After all, He is your Heavenly Father and only wants the best for you.

Slice 4: When in Doubt, Talk it Out

My entire life I've only had a handful of people I could tell all my secrets to. I could only trust a few people with my hearts desires and deepest thoughts. Sometimes it feels like we shouldn't be thinking certain things or feeling a certain way towards the opposite sex, but trust me, it's natural. Knowing how to act when we start to think about sex is very important. If we isolate ourselves with our thoughts and feelings, this could potentially lead to engaging in acts that may cause shame and embarrassment.

To save yourself the shame of partaking in sinful acts of the flesh, i.e.: fornication, pornography, and/or sexual intercourse before marriage, consider the following: utilize the resources you were given. Talk to a friend about how you're feeling and what you think you might do in a weak moment. Recruit an "accountability buddy". This person may be a close friend, a relative you trust or even someone you're not very close to but value their advice and opinions. Ask them to keep you accountable by checking on you and making sure you're steering clear of sexual temptations. There are even accountability apps, so if you have a cell phone, tablet or another handheld device, consider downloading one of the accountability apps if you feel it could help you stay on the right track.

Some of the available apps are Accountable2You, EverAccountable, CovenantEyes, and Pure. There are many, many others available for all types of phones and devices, but some of these actually keep you accountable by tracking what you search for and what you view. If you begin to view something that is inappropriate, an alert will pop up and sometimes be sent to your accountability partner. In my opinion, this could be one of the best ways to utilize the internet.

I can honestly say if I had someone to talk to who wasn't engaging in sexual activity before marriage, I might not have given in so easily at such a young age. Find someone you know who has good morals and standards that you look up to so that you can learn from them and go to them when you need support. This person will keep you from making a mistake that will change your life forever; no matter how "small" the act. Count yourselves blessed if you have parents or guardians who are open and willing to listen to you and not judge you. I never felt like I could go to my parents with issues regarding sex because it simply wasn't talked about. Find someone you can confide in; it can only ensure your success in this area of your life.

Ecclesiastes 4:9-12 "Two are better than one; because they have a good reward for their labour. For if they fall, the one will lift up his fellow: but woe to him that is alone when he falleth; for he hath not another to help him up. Again, if two lie together, then they have heat: but how can one be warm alone? And if one prevail against him, two shall withstand him; and a threefold cord is not easily broken."

I had amazing friends who were always there for me whenever I needed them, but they all lost their virginity by the age of 14, so in a way, I felt like I needed to do the same in order to be able to relate to them. I wanted to be on the same "level" as they were. I didn't like feeling as if I was being left out. I guess I was sort of a follower, but I knew I could make my own decisions. Eventually, sex became something that you just did when you're dating. It was almost expected after a week or so of dating someone. It was as if you completely forget that sex is meant to be something special that married couples get to enjoy. It became something that was almost as casual as greeting someone with a handshake. No meaning, no feelings, and no love. There was nothing spiritual or emotional about it; and looking back, it breaks my heart to know I went completely against God's plan for physical intimacy. God places people in our lives to teach us something; whether it's by their words or by their actions. It's up to us to decipher how we want to use those lessons. I could have seen the actions of my friends as actions I didn't want to mimic. Instead, I chose to follow their lead and enter into meaningless relationships.

So finding someone to confide in and lean on for support who has decided to wait until marriage to be intimate is the key. I can't say it'll be easy to talk to someone about sex, but I can assure you that if you find the right person to talk to, you won't regret it. Surround yourself with people who have high standards and are willing to be the support you need; and as always, keep God first and He will protect you from making mistakes that will leave a lasting impression in your life.

"*Daring greatly means the courage to be vulnerable. It means to show up and be seen. To ask for what you need. To talk about how you're feeling. To have the hard conversations.*" *-Brene Brown*

Slice 5: Dating with a Purpose

You may have noticed that I refer to my childhood a lot, but as I look back, I see several areas that I could have definitely used better guidance and boundaries. One thing I want to instill in my children is that marriage is forever. I also want them to understand and believe for themselves that intimacy before marriage usually leads to a lot of pain and regret. I used the word "usually" because there are those select few couples who engaged in sexual activity before marriage and actually ended up marrying and are still together today. In most cases, that isn't reality.

Dating with a purpose is something I heard within the past few years that makes me, as a mom, a bit more relieved when it comes to thinking about my children entering into the dating phase of life. Dating with a purpose means having marriage in mind when seeking out that special someone you want to spend more time with. The dates are supervised by an older friend or relative and the time spent together is a time to talk and get to know one another. When you start to view someone as a possible spouse, that thought alone will cause you to analyze things you may not have if you were simply dating because it's "fun" and what everyone else is doing.

I started dating when I was thirteen years old. My son will be thirteen next year and there's no way he will be allowed to date by then. I secretly had boyfriends that my parents didn't know about, but they did know about them by the time I was fourteen. I know my parents wanted me to be happy and they did the best they could with what they knew how to do, but what I really needed were boundaries while my hormones were running rampant. Even as adults we need boundaries; they make us feel safe and secure. Without them we do things that we normally wouldn't do; sometimes because of peer pressure, other times, simply because we can.

"Dating with no intent to marry is like going to the grocery store with no money. You either leave unhappy or take something that isn't yours." -Jefferson Bethke

When I was 14, I dated a guy who was 21 named Kevin. I told my parents he was only 17 and surprisingly, they believed me. Up until then I didn't give my parents any reason not to trust me, so I can see why they took my word for it. I don't remember how I met Kevin, but looking back I shudder at the reality of the situation. Not only was he a pedophile, he was also a gang member. I didn't know what the consequences of getting involved with a person like this would be, nor did I really care because heck, here was an older guy who took interest in little ole me, *and* I was impressing all of my friends by dating someone much older than me.

One of the very few days I actually spent with him has been imprinted in my mind as if an old French wax seal stamp was used to place it there. My sister dropped me off in front of his house; which was a white, dilapidated, shack of a house. She didn't want to leave me there but I insisted it was ok. She left as I went inside. I wasn't greeted at the door like a nice gentleman should do when inviting a girl to his home. I saw him sitting in a chair on the phone with what sounded like a girl. He promised it was his "cousin" but judging by the conversation he was having with this girl, this was no cousin; and if she was, I should've used that as my opportunity to hightail it outta there. But, I didn't. I stayed. When he got off the phone, we talked and eventually ended up in his room. He attempted several times to persuade me to have sex with him but I declined every time. He (thankfully) stopped and decided to invite his two dogs into the room which were two of the largest dogs I have ever seen, even to this day. I was terrified of dogs and he thought it was funny. Again, another opportunity to leave. But I stayed. We decided to take a walk to his grandma's house where his family was preparing to have dinner. I met his two sisters, his mom, dad, and grandparents. They all kept staring at me and I couldn't figure out why. I know now why they were staring: I was a child!

After meeting everyone, he wanted to walk back to his house but I decided it was time for me to leave. I asked him to find someone to take me home and finally he asked one of his sisters to drop me off. He seemed mad but I didn't care. I just wanted to be home, where I felt safe. I had actually been "dating" him for a couple months before this incident but after that day, I knew I needed to break up with him. I ended up telling my parents that he was actually 21 years old and that I was afraid of him. Kevin ended up calling my house and my dad answered and told him to never call again and to leave me alone.

Later, I received a call from his friend telling me that Kevin was planning to do a drive-by shooting on our house. I was so scared and so ashamed of the situation I put my entire family in that I actually prayed for protection around our home and my family. I am eternally thankful that God protected us from something horrific happening, all because I decided to be selfish and become involved with a dangerous person. Although this experience is a bit on the extreme side, I hope you'll realize how dangerous dating without a purpose (and at such a young age) can be.

After losing my virginity (to the boyfriend I had after dating Kevin) and dealing with the issues of being a single teen mom, it became easier for me to engage in sexual activity. I began to lose sight of the "perfect family" I had always wanted. In a way, my outlook on life was tainted. I wanted to hurt guys like they hurt me. I thought I had it all in control and I was the one calling all the shots, when in reality, I was only hurting myself. I was the one who, at the end of the day felt ashamed and used.

Dating without a purpose usually ends in hurt feelings, anger, resentment and shame. Almost every relationship I had before I married my husband ended up in tears. I entered into relationships knowing that I wasn't going to marry that person. I continued down the same path, with the same type of guys until I felt so ashamed of how I was living. God did not intend for us to have broken relationships, regret, and scars from our past. I really like how Sue Bohlin said, "Sexual purity before (and during) marriage prevents "ghosts" in the marriage bed; comparisons are nowhere as deadly as in the intensely intimate realm of sex."

When we date without a purpose, we go against God's perfect plan for a sacred and holy union between man and woman. In order to avoid bringing pain, wounds and scars from past relationships into a marriage, we must keep God first in every relationship. By doing so, He will lead you to the man that He has set aside just for you.

Jeremiah 29:11 (NIV) "For I know the plans I have for you, declares the Lord, plans to prosper you, and not to harm you, plans to give you hope and a future."

Slice 6: Concealed in a Box

1 Peter 3:3-4 "Whose adorning let it not be that outward adorning of plaiting the hair, and of wearing of gold, or of putting on of apparel; But let it be the hidden man of the heart, in that which is not corruptible, even the ornament of a meek and quiet spirit, which is in the sight of God of great price."

We all know that pizza comes in a box. It's usually brown with the company's name on top. We also know what's inside of those brown boxes. When the box is opened up, everyone rushes to see and smell the deliciousness that they will soon be eating; making it nearly impossible (even for someone on a diet) to keep from taking a slice.

Don't worry, I'm not saying women should walk around looking as plain and dull as a pizza box. Nor am I saying that it's a woman's fault if a man attacks her because of her choice to dress immodestly. What I am saying is that we should adorn ourselves in such a way that a man can look at us without committing sin in his heart. The ability to abstain from sexual activity is much harder once we've seen more than we should have.

It is our responsibility as women to keep our bodies covered up so that a man will want to get to know our heart before wanting to uncover it. Remember ladies, men are much more easily aroused by sight than women are! Revealing what God has given us sends the message that you're available and open to being looked at and lusted after; which is not what the Lord desires.

"You can dress attractively without being immodest. Within the Lord's guidelines, there is room for you to be lively, vibrant, and beautiful both in your dress and in your actions." -Thomas S. Monson

"When a woman veils her body in modesty, she is not hiding herself from men; She is revealing her dignity to them." -Unknown

"My idea of sexy is that less is more. The less you reveal, the more people can wonder." -Emma Watson

"Modesty is...a wall to the uninvited, a guardian to what is protected, an invitation to the respectful, a statement of values to the

unbeliever, a sense of dignity to the culture that wages war on our worth, and a gift of honor to the One we represent." -Shara McKee

The last quote brings tears to my eyes and couldn't have been said better. Not only does the way we dress show others what we're all about, but it shows that we represent an amazing God whom we respect and glorify with our bodies. *1 Corinthians 6:20 says, "For ye are bought with a price: therefore glorify God in your body, and in your spirit, which are God's."*

1 Timothy 2:9-10 "In like manner also, that women adorn themselves in modest apparel, with shamefacedness and sobriety; not with broided hair, or gold, or pearls, or costly array; but (which becometh women professing godliness) with good works."

Modest: having or showing regard for the decencies of behavior, speech, dress, etc.; decent.

Shamefacedness: modest or bashful.

Sobriety: temperance or moderation.

*1 Two young ladies arrived at a meeting wearing clothes that were quite revealing. The Chairman took a good look at them and said, "Ladies, everything that God made that has value in this world is well covered, hard to see, find or get."

He went on to say, "Where do you find diamonds? Deep down in the ground, covered and protected by the earth's soil."

"Where do you find pearls? Deep down at the bottom of the ocean, covered up and protected by a beautiful shell."

"Where do you find gold? Way down in the mines covered over with layers of rock. To find gold, you have to work hard and dig deep down to get to it."

He looked at them with serious eyes and said, "Your body is sacred and unique. You are far more precious than gold, diamonds and pearls and you should be covered too. If you keep your treasured mineral just like gold, diamonds, and pearls, deeply covered, a reputable mining organization with the requisite machinery will fly down and conduct years of extensive exploration before attempting to dig up your precious jewels. First, they will contact your government, (family) sign professional documents, (wedding) and mine you professionally (legal marriage). But if you leave your precious minerals uncovered on the surface, you will always attract illegal miners to come and mine you illegally. Keep your bodies deeply covered so that you only invite the professional miners to chase you."

Ladies, this couldn't be more true! If we attract the wrong kind of attention, from the wrong guy, guess what we'll end up with? The wrong guy who gives us the wrong attention and will most likely treat us the wrong way! If you wait on God, He will bless you with the right man who will get to know your heart before taking your precious jewel.

*1-Credit due to Grand Motivation Squad

My husband has told me many times that he values the fact that I dress modestly because my body is meant to be seen solely by his eyes. When a man sees a woman dressed modestly, it shows them that you demand to be respected. I urge you to consider keeping your body covered up and only revealed to the man that God has hand picked just for you. If it's something that you struggle with, bring it to God in prayer and I truly believe He will help you to understand why we should dress modestly.

Slice 7: Sharing is Not Caring

As children, we are taught that when we share, it means we care. That is true when it comes to sharing our toys, food, clothes, etc.; but it couldn't be more false when regarding sharing a slice of your pizza before marriage.

I came across this quote while doing some research on sexual purity: *"Biblical prohibitions are intended to protect something precious, not deny something pleasant." -John Piper at DesiringGod.org*

Children are given rules and boundaries that they are expected to follow. If they don't abide by those rules and stay within those boundaries, what happens? They end up getting hurt or put in the corner to stare at the wall for five minutes. They learn rather quickly, (some do anyway) that there are consequences to their actions, and there are prizes/praises to their obedience.

When it comes to partaking in sexual relationships before marriage, the harsh consequences one may face could be life threatening. There are numerous STD's (sexually transmitted diseases) that could greatly hinder the future you hope to have with a spouse. Some of these could cost you your life. Many have died from AIDs, and thousands still suffer daily from the choices of their past.

Another consequence of premarital sex is teen pregnancy. I believe every child is a gift from God regardless of how they were conceived; but since I had a baby as a teenager, I realize this is not the ideal way of starting a family. According to cdc.gov, in 2013, a total of 273,105 babies were born to women aged 15-19 years. When an unplanned pregnancy occurs, there are several options the expectant mother may choose from. Of course the choice to keep the baby and raise him/her should be the number one choice, but, unfortunately, it isn't always what the mother or family wants. Adoption is the second best choice. The last choice is one that I do not agree with no matter the circumstance, which is abortion. Each of these choices have their own set of struggles that are completely unavoidable, but abortion carries the most weight.

When I was 17 years old, I met a guy who was a "friend with benefits" type of guy.

It was only a physical relationship. I didn't have feelings for this person, nor did I think he had feelings for me. One night when we were together something happened and the form of protection we used was no longer reliable. The next morning I confided in a friend and told her what had happened and I needed to make sure that I did not end up in an unplanned pregnancy. She picked me up and drove me to the nearest Planned Parenthood facility where they rushed me in and gave me the "Plan B" pills. Now, although I can't say for sure I was pregnant, there was a very good chance I could have been. I chose to stop any chance of life forming inside of me. I regret that it was so easy for me to make that quick decision, and I greatly regret making the decision to have a physical relationship with someone that I didn't care about. Someone I never intended to marry.

If you, or someone you know, has found themselves in an unplanned or unwanted pregnancy, there is help available. There are pregnancy crisis centers ready and willing to help with prenatal, parenting and sexual integrity classes. They also provide opportunities for women and young ladies to "purchase" items for their unborn babies.

They can also assist young moms who do not wish to keep the baby, to get ready for placing the baby up for adoption. There are always waiting parents who aren't able to conceive a child on their own, so adoption not only helps the expectant mother, but it blesses a couple who are more than willing to care and love for a baby. If I knew about a pregnancy crisis center when I became pregnant at the age of 15, I would have definitely used that resource to learn all that I could about my changing body, the growing baby inside of me, and to collect items I would need to care for him to help lighten the load off of my parents.

In 2009, I volunteered at a pregnancy crisis center in Sonora, California. I became a Client Advocate and I taught prenatal, parenting, and sexual integrity classes. One of my youngest clients was 15. She was due with a baby girl right after her 16th birthday. Coincidence? I don't think so. I received a call from the receptionist as soon as this girl showed up at the center. Our receptionist thought of me instantly because of what she knew of my past. I left home right away to meet her and her mom. There were a lot of tears and hugs, but when the meeting was over, she decided to keep her baby.

(Although, I'm sure the thought of abortion never crossed her mind.) I never got to meet her little girl, but I do know that I was meant to be there for such a time as that. If she (or her parents) would have chosen to take that baby's life, she would have had to live with a lifetime full of guilt, shame, and regret. The effects of abortion don't just disappear when they take the baby away. Some of the physical side effects from an abortion are abdominal pain and cramping, nausea, vomiting, diarrhea, spotting, and bleeding. Some of the risks of having an abortion are heavy or persistent bleeding, infection, sepsis, damage to the cervix, scarring of the uterine lining, perforation of the uterus, damage to other organs and death.

Aside from the physical side effects of having an abortion, the psychological effects consist of issues such as eating disorders, self inflicted harm, self hatred, depression, anger and so on. According to abortionfacts.com studies have shown that after 8 weeks of an abortion 55% of the women studied expressed guilt, 44% complained of nervous disorders, 36% had experienced sleep distrbances, 31% had regrets about their decision, and 11% had been prescribed psychotropic medicine by their doctor. Psychological effects from an abortion could last a lifetime and greatly alter one's future.

In a study of teenage abortion patients, half suffered a worsening of psychosocial functioning within seven months after the abortion. Symptoms included: self-reproach, depression, social regression, withdrawal, obsession with the need to become pregnant again and hasty marriages. Women who have undergone counseling after an abortion report over 100 major reactions to the abortion. Among those reported are: depression, loss of self-esteem, self-destructive behavior, sleep disorders, memory loss, sexual dysfunction, chronic problems with relationships, dramatic personality changes, anxiety attacks, guilt and remorse, chronic crying, flashbacks, loss of interest in previously enjoyed activities, and difficulty bonding with children born to them later on.

According to hhs.gov, teen parents are less likely to finish high school, more likely to rely on public assistance, more likely to be poor as adults, and more likely to have children who have poorer educational, behavioral and health outcomes over the course of their lives than do kids born to older parents. Why is this? Teenagers are still kids themselves! They still need their parents and/or caregivers to provide for them. They do not have the mental, emotional or financial capacity to care for and raise a child.

Dosomething.org says, 8 out of 10 teen dads don't marry the mother of their child. I am part of that statistic. Let me say this, I have such admiration and respect for single moms! You are amazing women and deserve to hear this daily. I have been greatly blessed with a man whom God placed in my life to not only love and care for me, but to love and care for my son as well. Ladies, I cannot say this enough, give your heart to God. He will protect it and only give you to someone who is worthy enough to treasure you like the precious gift you are.

Slice 8: Created to be Enjoyed

I have yet to meet someone who hates pizza. I've heard people say it isn't their favorite food, but they'll still eat it if offered a slice. Pizza was created to be enjoyed; as was sexual intimacy between married couples. Most people have had different experiences regarding both pizza and sex, but one thing's for sure: they were created to be enjoyed.

I'm sure you've seen movies where "Christian" parents talk to their kids about sex being bad. They think that if they paint a picture of sexual intimacy being *bad*, then maybe their kids won't want to partake in it before marriage; but all this does is cause confusion. As a married woman, I can say that sex is not bad. In fact, it is meant to be greatly enjoyed. If it wasn't enjoyable, then it would only be meant for reproduction. Not only is it permissible, but it is also holy. When a man and a woman are married, they are presented with this beautiful gift from God that they can share with one another for the rest of their lives.

Ecclesiastes 9:9 "*Live joyfully with the wife whom thou lovest all the days of the life of thy vanity…*"

In Song of Solomon, King Solomon himself describes perfectly God's intention for a husband and wife's sexual relationship. Solomon makes it clear that a man has the freedom to enjoy his wife's body and vice versa. In Song of Solomon chapter 7 he says, *"How beautiful are thy feet with shoes, O prince's daughter! the joints of thy thighs are like jewels, the work of the hands of a cunning workman. Thy navel is like a round goblet, which wanteth not liquor: thy belly is like an heap of wheat set about with lilies. Thy two breasts are like two young roes that are twins. Thy neck is as a tower of ivory; thine eyes like the fishpools in Heshbon, by the gate of Bathrabbim: thy nose is as the tower of Lebanon which looketh toward Damascus. Thine head upon thee is like Carmel, and the hair of thine head like purple; the king is held in the galleries. How fair and how pleasant art thou, O love, for delights! This thy stature is like to a palm tree, and thy breasts to clusters of grapes."*

While doing some research on sex being a gift from God, I came across a Family Life article that I found quite helpful. Here are some interesting points I couldn't help but share:

-The Bible talks more about enjoying the pleasures of sex than it does about being fruitful and multiplying. Dr. Ed Wheat wrote, "God Himself invented sex for our delight. It was His gift to us-intended for pleasure." Along with the physical benefits of intimacy in marriage, there are spiritual and mental benefits as well.

-Physical intimacy between married couples is much more than a physical act that ends within a few moments. Sex brings two people as close as they can possibly get in body, soul and spirit.

Every sexual experience I've had in my past doesn't even come close to the intimacy I have with my husband. I never felt connected to anyone in my past, and after getting married, I finally understood why. The intimacy between a married couple is far more spiritual than most people realize. God intended for that union to be spiritual, just as He intends our union with Him to be spiritual. The Bible is a long love story about God and His bride (church). He likens the marriage between man and woman to the marriage of God and His Church. Ephesians 5:25 says, "*Husbands, love your wives, even as Christ also loved the Church, and gave himself for it.*"

1 Corinthians 7: "*Now concerning the things whereof ye wrote unto me: It is good for a man not to touch a woman. Nevertheless, to avoid fornication, let every man have his own wife, and let every woman have her own husband. Let the husband render unto the wife due benevolence: and likewise also the wife unto the husband. The wife hath not power of her own body, but the husband: and likewise also the husband hath not power of his own body, but the wife. Defraud ye not one the other, except it be with consent for a time, that ye may give yourselves to fasting and prayer; and come together again, that Satan tempt you not for your incontinency.*"

This scripture makes it very clear that sex is for married couples. Paul was stating to direct our sexual desires towards our spouse and make sure that our spouse is "fulfilled" or happy in this area. If there wasn't a need to be satisfied in this area of our lives, then it wouldn't have been made pleasurable. God created sex to be a bonding experience between married couples. He designed us to be physically driven to one another, so He created intimacy as a way for couples to fulfill the sexual desire that is both physical and spiritual. As a married, Christian woman I can honestly and wholeheartedly say that physical intimacy is far more spiritually and emotionally bonding than the mere act of premarital sex.

If you're someone who has given in to sexual temptation, no matter what it was, I want you to know that it isn't too late to decide to remain pure until your wedding day. Through the power of repentance, there is forgiveness. 1 John 1:9 says, *"If we confess our sins, he is faithful and just to forgive us our sins, and to cleanse us from all unrighteousness."*

Isaiah 43:25 *"I, even I, am he that blotteth out thy transgressions for mine own sake, and will not remember thy sins."*

Ephesians 1:7 *"In whom we have redemption through his blood, the forgiveness of sins, according to the riches of his grace."*

2 Corinthians 5:17 *"Therefore if any man be in Christ, he is a new creature: old things are*

passed away; behold, all things are become new."

The night I laid in bed sobbing, repentance was taking place. I was begging God for forgiveness. The Bible tells us that whatever we ask in His name, it shall be done. I was forgiven and made new. I was given a fresh start. A chance to reclaim my life. That same forgiveness can be yours if you only ask. Jesus wants to forgive you and make you a new creature in Him. If you feel bound and heavy laden from your past, go to God in prayer and He promises to forgive you and set you free.

Waiting until marriage should not be viewed as a "bad" or "uncool" thing. Making the decision to be abstinent until marriage isn't always easy, but it shows others that you value and respect yourself. Sexual purity is a treasure meant to be guarded and valued. So you see, girls really are like pizza. The more slices you give away, the less you'll have to offer to the one you marry. God intended for the "sharing of pizza" to be between married couples. I pray that the words from this book have been rooted deep into your heart and that you will decide to give God all control, and decide to remain

pure until the day He has set aside for when
two become one; then, and only then, should
you share as many slices as you'd like.

My Promise to God

Dear Lord,

I give you my heart, my mind, and my soul. Guide my life as I seek to please You. Help me to glorify You with my thoughts, my words, and my actions. I trust that You will protect my heart, and will only release it to the man you have set aside for me. Surround me with people who will hold me accountable for my actions. Bless me with friends that I can trust and talk to when I need advice. Help me to abstain from sexual temptation by protecting my eyes, my ears and my heart from a world full of sin. I promise to remain pure and keep my precious gift hidden deep inside until that blessed day when I marry the one you have prepared for me. In the precious name of Jesus, I pray, Amen.

Psalm 139:14 "I will praise thee; for I am fearfully and wonderfully made: marvelous are thy works; and that my soul knoweth right well."